THE LOST COSMONAUTS

KEN HUNT

Book*hug
2018

The production of this book was made possible through the generous assistance of the Canada Council for the Arts and the Ontario Arts Council. Book*hug also acknowledges the support of the Government of Canada through the Canada Book Fund and the Government of Ontario through the Ontario Book Publishing Tax Credit and the Ontario Book Fund.

 Canada Council **Conseil des Arts** for the Arts **du Canada**

Funded by the Government of Canada — Financé par le gouvernement du Canada

 **ONTARIO ARTS COUNCIL** **CONSEIL DES ARTS DE L'ONTARIO** an Ontario government agency un organisme du gouvernement de l'Ontario | Canadä

Book*hug acknowledges the land on which it operates. For thousands of years it has been the traditional land of the Huron-Wendat, the Seneca, and most recently, the Mississaugas of the Credit River. Today, this meeting place is still the home to many Indigenous people from across Turtle Island, and we are grateful to have the opportunity to work on this land.

LIBRARY AND ARCHIVES CANADA CATALOGUING IN PUBLICATION

Hunt, Ken (Canadian poet), author
        The lost cosmonauts / Ken Hunt.

Poems.
Issued in print and electronic formats.
ISBN 978-1-77166-459-2 (softcover)
ISBN 978-1-77166-460-8 (HTML)
ISBN 978-1-77166-461-5 (PDF)
ISBN 978-1-77166-462-2 (Kindle)

        I. Title.

PS8615.U6785L67 2018   C811'.6   C2018-905765-3
                                    C2018-905766-1

Printed in Canada

> "…*the lens of my unskinned*
> *soul, opening to the void,*
> *is carelessly dissolved.*"

– Jalāl ad-Dīn Muhammad Rūmī

(*Dīvān-e Šams, 649*)

for
explorers
of the
dark

I. APOSTLES OF ICARUS

Apostles of Icarus lost
in last copies of documents
offered to secret pyres.

Sifting for heroes,
we pan carbonized remains
for golden flakes of ash.

From the waxy white
of faded snapshots, digitized
and archived, stare the eyes
of pride's resolve,
preserved by a second
capturing of light.

The nameless fascinate the named;
pharaohs erased for their follies,
soldiers, their graves unknown,
many, but of one monument.

We haunt radio telescopes, ghosts
to the stars we sieve for patterns
to call voices, pitching our eulogy
at would-be conquerors.

The shield of the Earth
sears our steel wings
as we fall home,
flirting with fire.

II. THE SPACE RACE

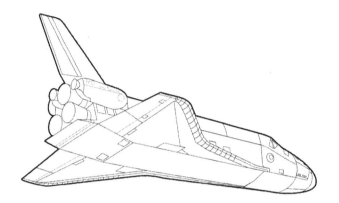

ENGINE

for Konstantin Eduardovich Tsiolkovsky

Grade schools refused a pupil marred by
scarlet fever, deafened by the virus,
as if time snagged his ears and amplified

their natural decay. Imposed silence
framed childhood vistas of frozen skies.
Rejection fostered an autodidact

and numeric artist, his recompense:
discovering a landmark equation
raised from the mulch of his readings. Intense

study revealed the key to Heaven's maze,
the mathematical passphrase for the
stern doors of sprawling ballrooms we have gazed

into since we put fire in reins. A sea
of magma parts for Rodin's gates, knowledge
twisting each self-imprisoned figure. We

struggle against the air we breathe, an edge
of caustic friction, amnion of flame,
while crammed into the cones of crafts alleged

to dethrone gravity. These structures tame
explosions violent as a tyrant's purge,
each craft sustained by its design, each frame

shaming predecessors. The boy emerged
a teacher, irony of ironies,
this student of himself. His brightly merged

imagination and constraint conceived
of steering thrusters, multistage boosters,
airlocks, and the rocket engine. Appease

the Hyades and Pleiades, lest Zeus
defend his kin, when launching these golems,
metallic guzzlers of rare fuels,

liquid O_2 and H_2 like silos
of chilled vodka, toasts to the sage who split
the beating organ of his youth before

a cold altar, in order to transmit
his dreams beyond his name, if we permit.

PROBES

Wayward voyagers
cast out from our lush harbours
glide over Titan.

Particles litter
their golden shells, pleas of Sol
infinitesimal.

Gloved hands assembled
these sterile machines with
gentle diligence.

Probes bathe in deep space
to capture faint snapshots of
ice caps made of wind.

One generation
monitors what another
began, each waving

like the parents of
gleaming offspring embarking
on dark odysseys.

CAPSULES

for Yuri Gagarin and Valentina Tereshkova

In your pre-flight portraits, your eyes are bleak as
rogue planets, your body strapped to a cage welded

to the steel palantir you will drive as far
from everyone as one can go. The deaths of your

comrades command your face, clamped in a muscular
pose of stoicism so complete, its opaque

repression of emotion compresses your fear
like the carbon of a diamond makes a mirror

of itself, revealing the weight you must carry
with you, like a second suit, as you breach the seal

of Tartarus, strapped to a burning bomb, hoping
the glitches that snatch lives will pass over you, the

door of your blackened cannonball tattooed with red.
Selected to gaze into the oubliette of

space, you find a maze so vast its edges remain
unseen. No trailing crumbs can trace trajectories

should you veer off course and stumble upon the ghosts
whose memories were burned away, but whose mobile

graves may outlast the Earth. Your eyes have aged beyond
you, as if trying to reconcile some damage deep

enough to creep to secret recesses, buried
as carefully as warheads. What ferocity

burns in those eyes, green as trinitite? Do they hide
as if in waiting to attack, to lash fury

upon the first to dare a glance? Even so, that gaze
could liberate the damned, could boldly infiltrate

abysmal gates, and with an unwinged gaze, could spill
warlight upon demonic denizens, demand

to free each flaming corpse from the sinuous straps
and veinlike wires laced to crackling seats, jockeys

tangled in their melting exoskeletons, their
faces fusing to the microphones we used to

monitor their spherical vehicles, as they
shattered our atmosphere in fugues of grinding fire.

As the strength of gravity recedes, tears of awe
collect beneath your eyes like sacs of dew. Friction

caresses blushing capsules, as if to woo the
metal to give up its structure, relent

to the gaping rage of chaos you hurtle toward,
drunken in this crusade to claim a plot of night.

STATION

Climb into a hive for humans, its modular corridors lined with ceramic to neutralize invading radiation. A new form of motion to frolic in, you are as weightless as breath. Bolted portholes give you pristine views of Earth, every horizon knit into a perfect arc

of clouds that hover above deserts vibrant in barrenness; over a sprawl of forest; over grasslands, stretching across fertile plains. Aboard, you become used to sleeping in a bag tied to the wall, a corpselike, vampiric creature, your body a pale frame. Dreaming machines, and the amplified rhythms of your heart and lungs ail the otherwise sterile quiet. A white leviathan's entrails surround you with guts of wire, tools, insulated ducts. The most pitiless wraiths of Hell would not dare haunt the vacant corridors of secret stations, orbits long decayed, left drifting

after their designers
destroyed themselves
with suns summoned
from deep below the
ground, for the spirits
of heroes guard, even

in death, these spaces
where they last stood
vigil, took commands
until unable to raise
their armoured limbs
to obey sacred oaths.

A lack of gravity will
atrophy your bones,
cause each muscle to
thin and slacken, let
your lungs succumb
to sloth, your blood
dilute. You will spend
hours exercising, but
you will still weaken.
Freedom from gravity
delimits you. Can we
survive, if space will

waste us all away, too
quick for our bodies
to adapt? How can we
afford to burn our sole
refuge when we have
no means of escape?
At the ISS station, we
examine ways other
forms of life adapt to
zero-g. A space-born
zinnia blooms, petals
the frail flesh of hope.

·

OFFSHOOTS

Eons pass. Posthuman progeny flee from a charnel house star system.
War and necessity reweave our skins; hardwired hatreds extirpated,
we ascend. No enemies thirst for our demise. Our collectives have thrived
stationed on poisoned moons. We built cities under Europa's ice crust, the

offspring of Atlantis. We scarcely resemble those who fantasized, while
they huddled at the anvils of resource wars, that they would achieve the stars.
Their forays were inane. Each world we terraform, offer to our offshoots,
becomes a beacon, an outpost for life and bulwark against entropy.

We took a cue from bacteria, viruses, prions and fungal spores,
each propogating with relentless diligence, building endurances
based on conditions encountered in arsenic badlands, in pools of
sulfuric acid, in caves the sun shunned for millennia. These little

nightmares gnawing at our backbones would pale as enemies, set against

our own outmoded biology, its crude processes abandoned, but

studied and archived, like out-of-date histories, laughable arguments

crippled by time. On the margins of galaxies, violent environments

bent on destroying us coax us to reforge our bonds. We are miners of

gas giants, asteroid plunderers, ruthless adaptors to shredding sands.

Four million years ago, Earth shook with fever and chills, as if infected

by our ancestors' stubborn efforts to propagate. How can we repent?

Composed of living language, we will inscribe ourselves upon the pages of

this brutal universe. Our imperatives will endure, as we transcend

physical boundaries, upload ourselves to self-maintaining servers, the

final nirvanas of consciousness. We have always yearned to shed our flesh.

III. VOYAGE TO LUNA

Come in, Houston. Recite for us the voyage of heroes who sailed an

ocean of vacuum as black as the pupils of Hades, in quest of the

ashen shores guarded by Artemis. Charged with this pilgrimage, Aldrin and

Collins and Armstrong each guided their craft past the edge of a scathing sky,

deep into primeval night, hoping they might gain Luna's favour and thus

spite Russian rivals by gracing her shores in a decade's time. Scouts braved the

vacuum, enabling the launch of the Apollo spacecraft, the eleventh

ship to shoulder so volatile a name, for the long-dormant rage of a

god can be jostled awake by the feeblest misstepping of mortals whose

arrogance narrows their sight. The first ship claimed the lives of its crew in a

sudden inferno that trapped them inside, Helios claiming overdue sacrifices owed to him for NASA's invocation of his Roman

name. With the edge of the decade approaching, the shipbuilders forsook sleep,

honed their arcane harnessing of the Titans' invisible forces, and

Florida's Cape, rechristened for Kennedy the betrayed, remained ablaze,

engines consuming fuel silos like flagons of wine at Olympian

banquets. Caffeine-driven technicians tweaked each design with geometry

salvaged from ages dissolved by the acids of time, while moon goddesses

watched from their pantheon carved in the wall of the crater called Korolev,

named for a Soviet engineer jailed in the Terror of Yezhov. His

life drained by slavery, Korolev's death gave advantage to Armstrong's crew.

Watching the mortals are Phoebe the Titan, grandmother of Artemis,

moon dust her war paint (essential for sacrosanct rites to derail fate);
and Selene, daughter of Titans Hyperion and Theia, sister of
Helios, who led her lover Endymion into unceasing sleep
at Latmus; Artemis also, the mistress of animals, daughter of
Demeter, huntress and stalwart protector, her snares full of comets, her
traps latched to alien beasts that must satisfy all the hungers of a
goddess of night; nearby Neaera, nymph of newborn moons and mother of
Phathusa, who traces designs in moon dust in front of the pantheon,
fingers precise as the pulses of water that mortals now use to cut
steel; Achelois, pain cleanser, who ruminates in her chamber of
moon rock that overlooks Korolev, scrying at mortals whose trials have

yet to be settled, whose actions will ripple for better or worse in the
ballads and tapestries capturing them; Hecate, haunter of dungeons, the
bearer of torches, the holder of keys, the necromancer, witchcraft her
mother tongue, poisons and herbal cures her secrets, spectres her collective;
Perse and Pandia, who bound down windless halls, newness and brightness, the
Moon's glow and cycle, their hair pluming outward, as viscous as reeds in a
honey-thick sea, their skin sugared with ice crystals. Lo! The eighth mission of
Helios approaches. Selene sees her Roman name label documents,
wiring, panels and newspapers, capsules and badges, an adjective
hopping the lips of the mortals, a chanting not heard for millennia.
Luna to *Lunar* to *Moon*, as if she were the sole goddess warding night.

Stirred by the sight of Apollo 8, each of the matriarchs drift to the
pantheon's innermost chamber, where silvery thrones cast in silicon
sheathe their luminescent skin, each cold chair inlaid with magnetite murals
depicting astral wars foreign to mortal lore. Phoebe, the wisest one,
muses to her sisters: "Mortals are dreamers of tragic absurdities,
destined to self-obsessed paths, their souls blighted with yearning and apathy.
We must extinguish this campaign of blasphemy, one bound to disgrace a
once-grateful people reverent of goddesses and gods alike. We once
guided the mortals; now they seek to conquer us. I'll not forgive them this."
"They are explorers, not arrogant conquerors," says Phoebe's niece, Selene.
"Violence is not their sole aptitude. Credit them for their pursuit of truth."

"They pursue truth as a hunter does prey," adds Artemis. She then plucks a silver feather from the hawk on her shoulder, the gleaming titanium beast wincing. "As if to simply ensnare such an animal teaches the hunter to sniff out its soul." The huntress flicks the feather, and Hecate glides from her throne, catching the glimmering trinket mid-spin. She twirls the treasure before her charcoal lips, wearing a long smile. She blows on the feather, transforming it into that of a mortal hawk and sliding it into her hair. She addresses the room. "Who are we to judge the hubris of the mortals? They punish themselves most effectively in their slow blunderings." Artemis sighs at Hecate's objection. "Mortals lack patience, cannot track truth without killing it, and they cannot learn, even from their worst errors."

Naera adds her voice. "Humans are fragile beings, their fears all but
infinite. Though they may blunder, their hearts are so soft it is wondrous
any have done what these voyagers and their armourers have. Are we so
callous we'll damn them for bravery? Are we so weak we'll be slaves to our
spite? I say let them land. It will inspire them more than they know it will."
Achelois remains silent, her auburn eyes reading the mortals, their
angst hidden from her kin. Hecate, now chuckling, sifts through her hair for the
feather, but pulls out a stylus, and studies the instrument. She does not
speak of this. Perse and Pandia then muse in unison, "Who cares what
we do? Our energy's better spent elsehow, our time better given to
dancing than caring for miscreant mortals, or should we say 'humans', as

Naera does, who forsakes our language in favour of blasphemy, *hmm*?"
Perse and Pandia snicker while Artemis raises her hand, and the
hawk on her shoulder opens its beak, loosing an eerie decree on the
vacuum. Artemis stands, grasping her bow, and fires an arrow at the
ceiling. Its tip clips the stone of the lunar room, sending the arrow's head
into the plinth at the chamber's core. Artemis glowers at Perse and
Pandia, now silent. "Focus. The eighth ship approaches us." Artemis
sheathes her bow, reclines, and clothes her brow with her hand. She then asks Selene to
retrieve the arrow now buried in the chamber's plinth. Selene drifts out to
fetch the projectile. As she does, Achelois utters scripture, a
quote of a quote from the crew of Apollo 8, spoken above the Moon.

"Darkness was upon the face of the deep." Hearing this, the council dissolves.

Each leaves the chamber to gaze at the orbiting mortals praying to them:

Borman and Lovell and Anders, each calling for blessings for all mortals.

Phoebe points out that they offer no sacrifice. Artemis shrugs at the

vessel, and calls the ship crude. Selene drifts toward the capsule, invisible.

Once inside, she peers through the window's narrow view, before approaching the

mortal men. Monklike in vigil, they maintain their vessel, preventing leaks,

adjusting oars, recording wave and weather, all while they commune with kin.

They navigate Luna's foreboding horizon, beseeching her with verse.

Perse and Pandia giggle. "They ask for blessings for all mortals

living, yet brandish no sacrifice? Laughable!" Achelois retorts:

"Journeying here is their sacrifice. They will continue, and if on their

eleventh voyage, they moor their craft gracefully, I'll grant the mortals my

blessing." At this, Phoebe scowls, her eyes flaming white, and vows never to

let any mortal set foot on such hallowed ground and escape back to Earth.

"Their armoured corpses will ornament our halls." Apollo 10 ferried

out Stafford, Cernan, and Young above Korolev, past the dark pantheon,

past Selene's bedchamber, past Hecate's laboratory, past the grasping gaze

cast by the beasts Artemis keeps beneath her room. When the eleventh ship

left the Earth, the huntress begrudgingly gave respect, though her leathery

soul offered Armstrong's crew no more pity than animals strayed from their den.

Each goddess watches the eleventh craft descend, a construct dependent

as much on fortune as on calculation. The ship runs aground in the
Sea of Tranquility, named for its favourable waters of dust. Inside,
Aldrin sips wine from a chalice. His gesture perplexes the goddesses.
"Does he mistake us for Dionysus's mad retinue?" asks Selene.
"No...this rite represents reverence for sacrifice," answers Achelois.
"Mortals give sacrifices to their gods. The reverse is mere blasphemy,"
spits Phoebe. When the hatch opens, the captain cannot escape, laden with
layers of armour. Artemis grimaces at this spectacle of birth.
Selene darts to the lander, placing her hands on the captain's air satchel.
Armstrong's heart gallops. He struggles to descend the vessel's ladder. Selene
shoves his satchel, freeing him. He climbs down to find gardens of feldspar and

andesite, minerals bloomed over epochs, and grasses of ashen dust
tended by meteorites. Hours later, Phoebe smirks as the mortal men
pilfer from this garden. "They come to rob and defame us, as I surmised.
When they attempt to leave, their oars will snap. They will die for this blasphemy."
Phoebe returns to the pantheon with her kin, all except Hecate, who
floats to the lander to find the two mortals staring at a broken switch.
Hecate retrieves her pen, kisses it, and slips the tool into Aldrin's hand.
Aldrin, his gaze torn away from his doom, holds the instrument out, and turns,
facing Hecate. "You think that'll work?" asks the captain, pointing at the pen.
Aldrin turns, blinking. He nods, and then slides the pen into the ship's panel.
Ignition commences! Upward the heroes fly, bound for their blue homeland.

IV. THE KARDASHEV
SCALE

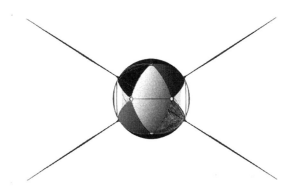

GLOBUS CASSUS
for Christian Waldvogel

Harvester ants transform their sand dunes, legions locked
in automated frenzies. Streams of drones connect
for shared imperatives, patrol their hoarded stocks,

protect languid queens that necessity elects.
Clamped in the vice of their design, these eager slaves
deliver larvae to the vaults they carve, dissect

the clay that blocks expansion of their sprawling maze.
Bewitched by instinct's chemical refrains, they race
to brace storerooms and passageways for the Great Rains.

Humans enact a plan to increase real estate.
Four sattelites grow toward the Earth. These progeny
of Babel reach halfway to Luna's doleful face,

with ductile needles of silicon, citadels
for Terra's oeuvre, soaring arks and archives knit
to house and to preserve, while we construct a shell

nourished by tendrils clad in graphene lattices
that siphon magma from our overburdened globe
into a vacuum-porous scaffold in orbit.

Centuries of construction change the dawn we share,
viewed through transparent sectors of silica glass
that invite sunlight to ideal plains and shores,

to empty seas conceived by architects to grasp
the fleeing hydrosphere of Terra, her mantle
coaxed away by infernal transfusion. At last,

we find the final gift of matter Earth will grant:
the cradle, sacrificed to shape its future urn,
presents its hoarded core of iron, for transplant

to complete an exo-Earth as wide as Saturn,
a bubble that captures Terra's vital weather,
the restless atmosphere that hovers, clots, and churns

above wildlife roaming vast, verdant reserves
and land masses conserved as artifacts, displayed
terrains to which pensive adventurers sojourn

from cities, the crowns of tailored horizons, made
to glean glimpses of Sol until we build his cage.

DYSON SPHERE

for Olaf Stapledon & Freeman Dyson

Entropy marks all empires with latent doom,
approaching, like an unseen hoard of fungal spores,
to envelop all matter in its creeping plume.

Scholars in halls carved from alien bedrock hoard
history's nectars in a hive of texts, for storms
of war must not reset our hourglass before

we grow into a strain of life that stalks the rims
of caustic seas, caretakers of bio-archives,
riding zip lines of spider silk over chasms

of extinction. How strange must we become to thrive
in space, to brace our anthills against astral rains?
When we have tamed our meagre star, will we still sigh

at the glow of engines moving homeward, a din
muted by the dark that promises familiar hearths
lie just ahead? Or will our grim indifference win

over our empathy, trampled under the march
of passing generations? Will our sentience
evanesce like pre-dawn mist above a vacant park?

The alms of our sun no longer meet the needs
of our machines, whose children we release to spin
a web to trap the star by which we were conceived.

Escher rendered a construct of concentric rings
rotating around a star, yet fixed like a mask
of machines, to snatch flighty photons and their kin.

Shadow-thin sheets of carbon repeat their task
of self-replication, swarming to form a shroud
around Sol, so the dawn will be distilled at last.

The veil thickens, caging Sol, a dragon cowed
by carbon spells. His muzzled flames enrich the land
we craft inside his prison egg, a brief abode,

since dragons' bellies swell with age, increase their span
the weaker their inner fires become. But far
from Sol, humanity maintains its long-term plan:

to populate the Milky Way, taming its stars,
and huddle near these lights, in vaulting abattoirs.

GALACTIC ENGINEERING
for Nikolai Kardashev & Peter Watts

Habitats forged from asteroid-salvaged ingots whirl
like dessicated spores, each mass of matter free
to drift in windless depths, outgrown by its builders,

beings that grow like crystals from incessant seeds,
and travel in amorphous hives, gorging matter
from planets, stars, and nebuli, their former deeds

faded from memory. Their ancestors' chatter
survives, archived as quantum bits and genetic
ciphers, embedded in living machines. Attar,

secreted by these flower-shaped monsters like sweat,
contains the secrets they received when they broke through
the barrier of self-awareness, fled the net

of sentience, a dead-end mutation, a slough
that, like La Brea's pits, ensnares its prey with fear's
endearing plea for flight, and doubt's insistent frown.

Freed from these glue traps for inferior species,
the builders flourish in soulless lucidity,
gamble adaptive drones in ploys without surcease,

analyze and smite their rivals, who grow livid
when they fail to bargain with demons for peace.
But the builders, met with extinction, would not give

out sentiment for monuments, or some secret
goodbye, embedded in a viral rose. Anguished
by his fate, did Orpheus ask Hades, or plead

for relief from sorrow, ponder relinquishing
all awareness of himself, all capacity
to feel? We have heard the murmur of this wish

near the radial Hells of black holes, accretion
discs whipping the runoff of malevolent suns
into flaming scimitars that guard creation's

knowledge, information that, when lost within, none
can retrieve unless they charm their way beyond the
singularity, a point clothed in warped light. Once,

this rift in physics riddled the builders, but free
of sentience's noise, their lyres were exact
in song, and led them on. The builders used to flee

from asteroids, lithic slag they worried would act
as fleets of warheads, eager to annihilate
their meagre populations. Prospective impacts

brought fear, stark as a stalking leopard's eyes, but fates
of mass death faded in the wake of more refined
tools. Their spears gave way to quantum-logic gates

that thought for them, processing the unkind
trajectories of errant slag, and running scans
of hypergiant stars that, at their grand demise,

must incarnate their bitter rage in spectral bands
so tightly packed, these gamma utterances sweep
galaxies away like murals of sacred sand.

But even these catastrophes of light and heat
the builders met with mirrored shields. They enclosed
outposts near stars prone to violent outbursts, greeted

each Medusa with its visage, each flaring boast
of rays from each dragon with coats of mithril rings.
Yet these galactic engineers are now, at most,

an echo of their ancestors, whose dreams and myths,
all glib, were figments of their flaws, mutations cloyed
with fragrant words of hope by literary smiths.

On the shores of the Eridanus Supervoid,
a well of eldritch depth all sentient life abhors,
our mindless children sip dark energy, deploy

their arts to probe dimensions beyond sense's doors,
the unexplored countries they toil blindly toward.

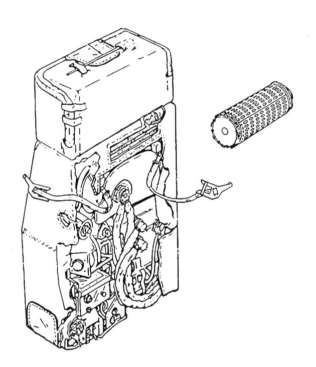

CRUCIBLE

for Valentin Vasilyevich Bondarenko

The glazed, saline lights of tears
glint as the sea burns with mirrored stars, fires
amid sunken lies, the ghosts of dead sparks.

An airbrushed photograph sparks
interest in hidden deaths, the shattered lights
of vacant rooms, filaments charred by fires
ambition lit, unlike those lightning burns
when forests crave renewal. Glowing tears
of cinder sprinkle blackened slag that lies

at hushed crash sites. Careful lies
conceal the horrors bred by stray sparks
in an oxygen-rich chamber. Hell tears
through dimensional barriers and lights
a cosmonaut. By Hades's spite, he burns
with flowing blossoms of infernal fires

gouging out his nerves. Pain fires
through dendrites, until endorphins tell lies
to his mind, blackened skin denied, his burns
fade amid innate, saintly guilt that sparks
his final words, an admission when lights
highlight his devastation. Panicked tears

choke through his rescuers. Tears
lacing his flesh glow with blood bright as fires
in star-edged badges, blazing like the lights
under which sombre censors weave state lies
thick enough to obscure the distant sparks
of covert launches, hinged on midnight burns

from foundry-born rockets. Burns
appear on cheeks nettled by restless tears
of lasting loss, a father felled by sparks
born of his careless act, flinging the fire's
catalyst toward his hot plate. No lies
may disgrace his monument. By the lights

that grace these frail pages, lights
imitating the star whose rising burns
away the night, these words mark one who lies
interred in engrams, freed from fitful tears
by reverent minds, spirit distilled. The fires
of synaptic snapshots hold his soul. Sparks

burst. Our dendrites' lights fix tears
in archived tomes. Burns edge a photo fires
met. The true self lies steeped in seas of sparks.

EYE OF DAWN
for the crew of Apollo 1

Distressed at the prospect of travel
in a vessel outfitted with an excess of flammable
materials, three astronauts mirror their palms
in sarcastic prayer, before a model of their
capsule, an ivory pyramid resembling

the marble-lacquered marker of Khufu's tomb.
This pharaoh's wizard, Djedi, designed
his god king's mausoleum to guide its principle
occupant (who sought in life the documents
of Thoth, god of knowledge) to the Netherworld,

where such secrets reside. Diagonal shafts
bisect cyclopean blocks of limestone,
inviting heaven's eyes to embalm sealed
chambers in celestial light, and granting
ghosts, lost amid their troves of treasures,

measured paths to meet their judgment. Captured
in monochrome atop a black table, the Apollo
capsule model hovers while the crew's bowed heads
and angled hands suggest that each man might
break into a bow before the snowy icon.

The crew, immersed in their chamber of pure oxygen,
could not see the liquid glycol coolant beneath their
feet react with silver-plated wires, to release electric
arcs. In minutes, solder joints melted. Spacesuits
fused to molten nylon. Investigators later found

a handprint, etched in ash, on the inside of
the hatch. In the sterile test facility,
technicians rushed past oxygen canisters
stacked like Canopic jars, the capsule window
glowing like the eye of Horus drawn wide.

COUNTDOWN
for Vladimir Mikhailovich Komarov
& Valentina Yakovlevna

Flight reduced his body to a grimace
of charcoal. His beloved's faintest touch
would have dismantled his crust of skin.

He kept faith in his parachute, trusted
a membrane designed to strain against
hellish speeds. But his tangled bundle

of fabric refused him. No radios could
sieve his dying calls from the muting
sheath of air that his capsule ionized.

His undiluted descent ended in a crash
like the hammer blow of a gavel held
in the wooden fist of a grisly judge.

This verdict emptied his beloved's bed,
transformed her haven into a foreign
landscape. After his landing, she dove

into the hush of Luna's placid oceans,
each a colossal urn for lost explorers.
At the Kremlin wall, his military knell

rang, before glinting officials entombed
his remains under grey stone. Three
crewmates, spared by their comrade's

demise, felt their bravery flicker like
a windblown flame. The sun undoes all
wax, the bees' sacred scaffolding, if we

misuse it in hubris. What fields of ash
must we sow amidst the arc of stars
in which we spin, our cabin corroded

by rabid wars, haunted by martyrs,
their deeds discarded? We deny that
each of us must face one final flight.

EZEKIEL 37:9
for the crew of Soyuz 11

Dobrovolsky, Patsayev, and Volkov docked
at Salyut 1, the first humans to moor a craft
in orbit. With their last transmission, the crew
encouraged their comrades on Earth to anticipate

toasts of hearty liquors to herald their homecoming,
and bid them gather sacred libations, complete with
an accompanying feast, a supper for those who passed
over all homes at unspeakable heights. The trio lacked

spacesuits, a measure their superiors agreed upon,
to save weight, space, and time during descent.
As they fell, a premature decompression left the crew
prepared for their embalmers. The capsule they shared,

once airless, acted as their sepulchre, before it bore
their bodies home, all else according to design. How
many ships have failed to shield their crews from storms
that compromised compartments, or from galling holes

that robbed each deck of breathable air? How many ghostly
galleons have drifted home, barges for the salt-crusted
corpses of starved crews? How many oars have snapped?
The Soyuz crew arrived in ghoulish repose, as if asleep,

their doll-like faces masks of false tranquility, framed
by thin trails of blood. If they had found the culprit
valve in time, a single finger placed over the leak would
have allowed all three to leave the capsule, to emerge after

inhabiting death's yawning maw for three long weeks,
to shed their white shrouds like Lazarus and live
on, as embodied icons of the miracle of space flight.
But, alas, at the landing site, medical personnel repeat

their futile ritual of CPR, their subjects only minutes
dead. Nearby stalks of grass, stiff as antennae,
receive a prophetic plea. *Come forth, four winds,*
and breathe upon these slain, that they may live.

FRAGMENT

for the crew of the Space Shuttle Challenger

Years later, on a Brevard County beach,
a mother gently shakes her daughter's

hand, dislodging a scrap of metal
from the child's grip.

Wary of potential infections, the mother
checks her daughter's palm and,

finding no mark, returns the child
to the family umbrella.

Lying near a Styrofoam cooler, the child
reflects on the texture of her artifact,

its surface smeared with the greasy
kiss of incessant heat, hallmark

of car parts and barbecues. The soft
gunshot of the pop can that dad hands out,

and the stinging cold of its aluminum shell,
brings to mind the shard's gnarled edge

and what force shored the fragment from
its greater whole. The dark jewel stood out

in the sand like a tree's last fallen leaf,
its surface browned and curled, as if decayed.

The pop and the shade fail to lessen
the loss of her treasure, so near to its finding.

The child pouts, but years later remembers
only sand crabs, skittering over powdered glass.

DARK MIRRORS

for the crew of the Space Shuttle Columbia

The Space Mirror Memorial has
room for 90 names on its wall of
black marble tiles, every name cut
out completely, through its tile,
allowing light to filter through a
backing of translucent acrylic, to
illuminate the names of the dead.
The wall once tracked Apollo's arc
and rotated, to keep its letters lit,

but when the mechanism failed, no
repair was made, in favour of a more
economical way of providing light.
Now, legions of artificial suns burn
behind this daunting monument,
day and night. An arc of white fence
encircles the towering grid of gold
and obsidian, gracefully barring all
visitors from touching the pristine

wall. Names adorn 24 tiles on the looming wall. Seven were cut when a piece of foam broke free, gashing *Columbia's* wing. Well-aware of her moulting, none expected a disaster, and so ignoring the phenomenon became the norm. How many more children, enraptured by their flight, must fall before Athena gives their

grieving parents wings? Daedalus,
ever bereaved, yet guiltless for the
warning that he gave. A new Icaria
lies far across the sea from Greece,
where all the craftsmen of NASA
could not kill contingency. Rename
the land for these fallen, each shore
a museum of unseen debris, each
wave whispering unheard eulogies.

CAUSALITY
for all apostles of Icarus

because defects in
electrical systems caused
apogee problems

because a goose smashed
through the cockpit, Plexiglas
clogging the engine

because the weather
disagreed with their intent
to test metal wings

because of a grievous
mechanical failure
in the aileron

because parachutes
may refuse to open like
stubborn buds in spring

because the pilot
veered to avoid tearing through
a weather balloon

because the water
of the Black Sea invaded
the cosmonaut's lungs

because the feathered
re-entry system deployed
prematurely

RED PHANTOMS
for the lost cosmonauts

May & November 1960:

> SOS signals
> trickle through the chrome mesh of
> scavenged microphones.

February 1961:

> Suffocating gulps
> ride air that their speaker's
> taxed lungs can't access.

April 1961:

> One spacecraft returns
> its pilot to Earth, the first,
> before Gagarin.

May 1961:

> A cosmonaut spins,
> circling the drain of space,
> his comrades silent.

October 1961:

> One craft glances off
> the atmosphere, its pilot
> a gift to the deep.

November, 1962:

> Instruments tremble
> in another ship that fails
> to rejoin the Earth.

November, 1963:

> A spacecraft consumes
> its pilot, who dies reading
> the heat of her tomb.

April, 1964:

> At friction's mercy
> a ship dissolves, its pilot
> a snowflake in spring.

VI. CELESTIAL BODIES

for Diane Ackerman

MARS, THE BRINGER OF WAR

Lone rovers thresh these empty continents and seas,
sandblasted basalt basins stained with ancient rust.

The blue sun staring through these raving skies laments
an atmosphere long banished by a stagnant core.

Pyroxene pikes and glaives of hazy glass protrude
from shallow valleys of volcanic olivine.

Across andesite and hematite expanses,
iron oxide gales enrobe ridges of feldspar

plagioclases in erosive embraces.
Lurid ballets of wind and grit on tainted stages

grind valorous ballads to violent halts, silence
the odes of jovial halls, crescendos shattered by

the tremors of advancing troops, the livid grains
whose gales clash on plains of battered silicates.

Each horde equipped with relics, weapons coaxed
from forges long gone cold, fashioned from molten streams

of distilled tectosilicates, tempered and honed
under unexplained auroras, crystals twinning

when these spectral legions reach collision, rivulets
of their souls coagulate in bladed waves that

wash across the face of Acheron Fossae.
The massacres geology retains confess,

in chronicles of rock, their fossilized bodies,
folded in wastelands pockmarked by astral buckshot.

At the summit of Olympus Mons, son of Zeus,
you clasp the arms of a throne constructed from limbs

of disassembled probes. Legions of damned below
poultice your loss of Venus with their agony.

♂

VENUS, THE BRINGER OF PEACE

Vulcan's eager lips hammer fissures into these
lobate lands, spawn flat-topped farra and arachnoid

fractures, features concealed by an insular
haze of carbon dioxide. Carrara white clouds

clothe roiling heavens in corrosive vapours that
could fast dissolve the flesh of falling astronauts,

or could erase, like Earthly rain, the sprawling glyphs
of chalk from sidewalks where a child spelt her dreams.

In spindrift gulfs, sulfuric acid rains baptize
angelic choirs, whose tortured cries echo across

calderas gouged from realms of sterilizing heat,
each open sore a doorway to the forge of Hell.

No folding of amino acids may profane
this virginal surface, may invade this veneer

of alabaster smog, may spill dark names upon
this cast of sacred plaster clotted over bone.

The balm that graced these desertscapes has vaporized,
leaving an atmosphere so dense that meteors

create no craters, lingering to contemplate
fatal caresses of assimilative flesh.

Photodissociated oceans expose beds
of fossils crushed to dust and sublimated in

volcanic volleys, ghostly imprints lost. Our probes,
like Aeneas, unable to embrace their shades.

In Ancient Rome, maidens revere love's avatar
with mint and rushes. Myrtle-crowned generals cleanse

blood guilt, speak *Venus Victrix*, and unwittingly
invoke the *venenum* of Aphrodite's wrath.

♀

MERCURY, THE WINGED MESSENGER

the bravest mote to
girdle old Apollo, this
courier of souls,
half-scalded by eccentric
orbit, dashes to
snatch divine communiqués,
rushes to catch nymphs
in spare moments, with stolen
nets, godly mischief unchecked,

                                    retreats, eclectic,
                                    into a cryogenic
                                    night, alternate face
                                    too cold to crack. Regoliths
                                    block sublimation
                                    of scattered sheets of frozen
                                    gases, moonlike skin
                                    stretches between the fractures
                                    criss-crossing the crust
                                    of this winged musket ball.

JUPITER, THE BRINGER OF JOLLITY

Anticyclonic vortices enrobe
a mantle of metallic hydrogen
in crystallized ammonia clouds, the hosts
of helium and neon rain. Lightning,

a thousand times the strength of Earthly strikes,
intrudes beneath blue aurorae that grace
each pole with flitting sprites of liquid sky,
the consorts of the eagles' aerial reign.

Amalthea's gossamer ring, a gown
of dust beyond the halo of her king,
suspends a senate of abyssal moons,
a flock fit for imperial auguring.

Caramel marble moulds a swirling eye
whose laws the fetial priest must valorize.

य|

SATURN, THE BRINGER OF OLD AGE

The rings of the City of Dis exist,
1.4 billion kilometres away.
Through treeless woods, we set our craft adrift.

The orb's north pole, a hexagonal rift,
a door to Babel's vaulting library.
In sleep, the reaping scythe of dream is swift.

The southern pole, a pit of shredding mist,
a vortex of chthonic revelry.
Through treeless woods, we set our craft adrift.

On shepherd moons, ichors of tholin shift,
assembling demons Hell could not allay.
In sleep, the reaping scythe of dream is swift.

Amorphous carbon litters moonlets kissed
by frost in each concentric ice ballet.
Through treeless woods, we set our craft adrift.

The severed wings of Cupid make a gift
for Lua Saturni, a chic entree.
In sleep, the reaping scythe of dream is swift.
Through treeless woods, we set our craft adrift.

♄

URANUS, THE MAGICIAN

rheumatic sun, again
unearthing a music, a
gam in chateau ruins,

a gunman heuristic, a
huntsman auric, i age
in aim, harangue cuts

in a much gaunt ear, is
a tune i am crushing, a
name uncaught, is air

at a churning, i amuse
amateurish cuing, an
inhumane act, i sugar

sumac, in a naughtier
uranium, as teaching

♂

NEPTUNE, THE MYSTIC

ice master's blind eye,
azure polished cataract,
and Kuiper's ward

> a colloquium
> of ocean deities soak
> beside this cold sphere

Naiad, the closest,
boasts intimacy, yet strays
toward her Roche limit

> second, Thalassa,
> crustacean mother of love,
> mermaid matriarch

Desponia, third,
daughter of equine mischief,
queen of mysteries

> fourth, Galatea,
> animated marble maid,
> the sculptor's android

Larissa, the fifth,
a hydria-bearing nymph,
heavily cratered

> the sixth satellite,
> s/2004 N 1,
> dark as fresh asphalt

seventh, Proteus,
lion, leopard, serpent, pig,
held by Menelaus

Triton, the eighth orb,
horn-bearing merman herald,
cryovolcanic

the ninth, Nereid,
like Diana's nymph, Opis,
slayer of Arruns

Halimede, the tenth,
Aegean spirit, storm balm,
crowned with red coral

the eleventh, Sao,
anti-siren, rescuer
of sea-damned sailors

Laomedeia,
the twelfth, a trident bearer
draped in silk and gold

Psamathe, thirteenth,
partner of Proteus, named
"Sand of the Seashore"

Neso, most distant,
most inclined, most retrograde,
a scream, cast in ink

♆

VII. ORBITAL DEBRIS

IN EVENT OF MOON DISASTER

Fate has ordained that the men
who went to the moon to explore in peace
will stay on the moon to rest in peace.

These brave men, Neil Armstrong and Edwin Aldrin,
know that there is no hope for their recovery.
But they also know that there is hope
for mankind in their sacrifice.

These two men are laying down their lives
in mankind's most noble goal:
the search for truth and understanding.

They will be mourned by their families and friends;
they will be mourned by their nation;

they will be mourned by the people of the world;
they will be mourned by a Mother Earth that dared
send two of her sons into the unknown.

In their exploration, they stirred
the people of the world to feel as one;
in their sacrifice, they bind more tightly
the brotherhood of man.

In ancient days, men looked to the stars
and saw their heroes in the constellations.

In modern times, we do much the same,
but our heroes are epic men
of flesh and blood.

IN THE SHADOW OF THE MOON
for Buzz Aldrin

I was open-minded
in anticipation watching
the earth grow smaller
the moon grow larger

but all of us were
totally surprised when
the larger moon
eclipsed the sun

we were in the shadow of the moon

satisfactory photographs
unfortunately
were not produced

the black sky was different
on the surface of the moon
from earth, the surrounding light
is visible when looking at the night sky

but on the surface of the moon
the sun's light gave
a pronounced velvet-like sheen
such that no stars were visible

the ambient light
enabled stars to be seen
through the telescope
but not through the visor
cover on the eyes

LAST WORDS

Prepare
cognac and sausage to go
with the moonshine.

See you tomorrow.

Roger, uh, bu–

Uh-oh.

Get us out.

It was my fault.
No one else
is to blame.

VIII. BEYOND THE
INFINITE

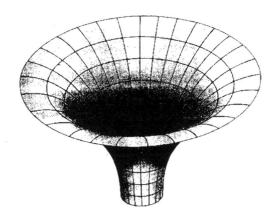

PALE BLUE DOT
for Neil Armstrong

They waved until their hands fell to their sides,
mild fatigue in wrists at rest, in preparation to enact
ritual motions on the craft's

precision instruments, each interface inspected
by meticulous technicians, all too cognizant
of conflagration, wracked by the chronicled
costs of unchecked flaws.

Screens, wiped clean each night, manifest
numeric narratives. Data projections coalesce.
Harmonies of half-concealed sighs invade control rooms.

Nemo's leagues recede into a jest, crammed
into seconds as ascent melds craft and blast
into a molten streak. Events are witness-forged.

Soaked with clinging wisps of wind, they left
the zephyrous crest whose lingering protects
the sprawling offshoots of an ancient spore,
vast droves of colonies in ceaseless conflict.

Life saturates itself and so, detached,
a single distant glimpse envelops and arrests
a multitude possessed by errant dreams

(mirror-induced paralysis).

Clinging mites mingle and scheme
on the battered crust of a molten globe
lodged in the unknown's numbing umbra
like a chalk outcrop atop the shores of Dover.

As wine-dark brine pummels
their porous refuge, they should shiver
like an animal, having isolated
itself at instinct's final call,
to be so near to nothing.

The daredevil flights of the few
lure them to a roaring edge where,
eyeless as Gloucester,
they ache for gravity's deliverance.

ASTRAL VAGABOND

for Muhammed Faris

Expatriates of a war-torn state flee
to nearby borders, families in tow,
a neo-exodus. Each one compelled
over some inner brink, sickened and laced
with terror and adrenaline, homeland

a fallen dream. For you, it was pilots
you trained, ordered to strike dissenters from
above, isolated and reprogrammed
to purge any hesitation. You failed to
escape three times, surveilled thoroughly,

too useful to lose. So you ventured out
on foot, one of the few who crashed through
the ceiling of the sky, now carrying your
future on your back, on a demented
family hike into permanent hiding.

What secret trails were you forced to take?
What grizzled contacts led your loved ones through
the underground, each numb with sleeplessness,
expecting familiar hands to clasp your
shoulders, haul you backwards as if you were

a disobedient child, scold you,
and put you back to work? The height of your
honour was a co-Soviet flight to
Mir, where your comrades proclaimed you hero,
member of the Order of Lenin. Now,

proclaimed a traitor, ripped from history, you see
your national accolades dissolve. You were trained
to endure the risks of ascent into space,
but nothing could steel you for the leap
from general to refugee. Even now,

you beseech your students of the skies to
relinquish their ranks and medals, emblems
of modern massacres, the badges of
the death of exploration, of an age
where we give up the stars, throw up our hands

and bow to grinning despots who convince
us we must fight our neigbours to survive.
Each new excuse for conflict forges new
divides, passed on like strands of viral genes
inherited with bloody infamy.

In myth, our heroes were our teachers,
in philosophy, our teachers heroes.
Reason and passion remain starved
for the same balm of hope with which we strive
to reach our rough-built destiny to rise.

SPACE POEM CHAIN
for Koichi Wakata

Floating before my eyes
in primordial blackness,

this blue, watery world
gave me life.

Thank you,
beloved.
You are
our home.

Tomorrow,
I am off again into
blue, unexplored worlds.

I will crack them open
for the dreams they hold.

Life obeys geometry, fan
blackmail in red prisons.

How dwelt subliterary
Eve? Elf magi,

thou yank
bold Eve.
Yea, our
moor hue,

to worm or
foaming ion, a fiat.
Exuded probes lull worn

ink, collect a whimper
of odes. Her myth held art.

ANTIVERSE PALINDROME
for Mikhail Pukhov

Spacecraft devouring space, accelerating
time, warping darkness. The tempered, supermassive
singularity the burgeoning engines wing

them to, distant Earth departed and impassive,
looms ahead. "Here we are," blares intercom after
intercom. Captain stoic and ship bolstered, last

out, and over shadows without form. Past spacecraft,
lost or wrecked, crews kindred in spirits, silenced
both captain and ship. This recollection surpassed

description. The portal that explorers and thinkers
all sought, has it destroyed all travellers? Binding,
infiltrating light, dim yet inviting, the rift

beckoning the spacecraft, antimatter churning.
The black, glowing veil, the closing frontier, the
antiverse mirror, their reflection. Trembling

and mumbling, their captain: "Now, die we may." He
and crew enter, time reversing, untethering,
modulating minutes and seconds like putty.

Navigator sees navigator, twins speaking:
"Reflections! We are–" always still, still and singing.

Singing and still, still always. "Are we reflections?"
Speaking twins: navigator sees navigator,

putty-like seconds and minutes modulating,
untethering, reversing time. Enter crew and
he: "May we die now?" Captain: their mumbling and

trembling reflection. Their mirror antiverse:
The frontier closing, the veil glowing black, the
churning, antimatter spacecraft, the beckoning

rift, the inviting yet dim light infiltrating,
binding travellers, all destroyed. It has sought all
thinkers and explorers, that portal. The description

surpassed recollection. This ship and captain, both
silenced spirits in kindred, crews wrecked or lost,
spacecraft past form, without shadows. Over and out,

last bolstered ship and stoic captain. Intercom
after intercom blares, "Are we here?" Ahead looms
impassive and departed Earth, distant to them,

wing engines burgeoning. The singularity,
supermassive, tempered the darkness, warping time,
accelerating space, devouring spacecraft.

THE PASSAGE LIES HERE
for Gwendolyn MacEwen

The passage lies here,
written in the lattice of iron knives
that hides behind the blackened skin
of a meteor fragment
submerged in the dust of Lacus Somniorum.

The passage lies here,
scrawled on the rims of lunar impact rings
we read as startled eyes
and mouths agape in a choir of screams.

The passage lies here,
emblazoned on capsules haunted
by vacant spacesuits,
sealed mausoleums diving on spiralling routes
through seamless black.

The passage lies here,
latched to the comets that score our probes,
fastened to the flares that tear themselves from Sol
like strips of rebellious flesh.

The passage lies here,
veiled by the plumes of steam
erupting from the pool beneath Saturn V
in the infernal echo of her maw.

The passage lies here,
disguised as a glint of iridium
on the polarized glass of a pair of aviators
stored in a war museum.

The passage lies here,
in the footnotes of a virus
straddling the copper strands etched
on the motherboards of the networked computers
assembled, like clay soldiers, in the data centres
of the NSA.

The passage lies here,
on the flag and family photo left
at the Apollo landing site, erased
by the gaze of the sun.

IX. PER ASPERA AD ASTRA

for Christian Bök

What happens to a species of explorers that have mapped their planet and set foot upon its moon, when these thresholds of successful conquest threaten to obliterate them? We have charted mountain peaks severe enough to thicken our blood for lack of oxygen, in order to capture pictures of ardent cloudscapes, Olympian vistas idealized in the surviving frescoes of Pompeii. We have sent machines on suicidal campaigns to volcanic vents that marinate their crustacean occupants in a miasma of sulfurous vapours. We have drilled boreholes into the depths of Siberian glaciers, in order to retrieve ancient bacteria. We have injected ourselves with untested cocktails of such motes, resurrected from their deathless slumber, but have gained no immortality from their presence in our blood. We have read the ongoing eulogy of the universe through the glass eyes of our satellites. We have clattered in cones atop exploding spires into the vaccuum we must always occupy, sacrificing the mystic innocence of our cosmic myths in exchange for sacks of moon rocks and shovelfuls of lunar dust. We have sent emissaries to puncture the dark, laden with summaries of our futility.

How many have spread their artificial wings only to reel, fire-torn, from their orbital thrones, or to careen on strayed trajectories into deep space? Was the first probe we hurled beyond the pull of our star the spherical coffin of a cosmonaut whose existence we erased for the sake of a race? If so, this sample of our mortality, this soul cast on an odyssey alone, like a lost kite hypnotized by wind, is the ultimate testament to our species. Life bereft of space suffocates itself, like the foliage that borders the jungled rivers that vent sweltering veldts, dense tendrils writhing to escape themselves, to steal sips of light from their neighbours. We have rebelled against the borders of our maps, which trap us with completeness, which encourage us to stagnate, which divert us from our purpose. We have seen fireflies fade in and out, the shared metre of their persistent beacons broken only by the dawn. Our mothers have knelt before stark walls of brick, adorned with portraits of their lost sons. Our officials have restrained these mourners in their woeful praying, as if such acts could exorcise the grief possessing them. Our capsules have come home, only to land off course, to snap through dark woods where emaciated wolves surround the cosmonauts trapped inside, and circle as night descends. These stranded voyagers have awaited the dawn, shivering as they never did in space. A test pilot emerged from his personal inferno, leaving his skin, his lips, his eyes behind, yet he has managed to utter to his rescuers an apology for being the cause of his demise. The final words of our species, if we have fostered in ourselves a sense of grace from our defeats, will echo this whispered admission of regret. The hands of the stopwatch that workers pan for, in the charred slag at the crash site of a capsule, the glass face of the timepiece blasted with grease and soot, will be frozen at the instant of impact. How can a species, content to remain the rabid cancer of its birth planet, hope to outlive even the overlooked crystalline growths that share its home, cthonic fauna that bloom unbidden and untended in their undiscovered catacombs, remaining hidden as they propogate, until the radius of Sol bloats, vaporizing their obsessive symmetries? We have been imprisoned in the mirrors we have cast. Our innards have been liquefied by the spiders we have engineered. The earthquakes of our making await us, the blackening of the sun by greenhouse fumes, the blood-red discolouration of the moon, the rain of stellar flak that splits the sky, the unrolling of history's final scroll, the collapse of all that we call strong. Who among us can stand against an indifferent universe? Would an encrypted letter, cast into the void, comfort us better than the act of writing it, a desperate yet effective consolation for the panic we must all deny, the by-product of our insipid gift of sentience? Writing distracts us from the agonies of mortality with a labyrinth of virtual realities. The music of these dreams is the means by which we dive into our intuition, star-eaten, in the deep repose of sleep: the final clang of a bell's black tongue on the roof of its rusted mouth, the auto-weaving pattern of spring frost on blocks of rotting masonry, the nuclear-powered eulogy of a long-dead species on an interstellar tour, the cavalcade of countless torments quarantined in the quarters of speech, the gardens of machines, the low chiming of lightning that clips the sky, and the candles that close out the night.

X. ESCAPE VELOCITY

THE LOST COSMONAUTS

Inventors of technologies later instrumental to space exploration, such as the Russian polymath Konstantin Tsiolkovsky, never imagined that their ideas would be appropriated for use as instruments of war. Daedalus, the mythical father of Icarus, similarly never imagined that his son would succumb to ignorance and arrogance, fly too close to the sun, and melt the wax wings so meticulously designed by his father to fly him to safety.

Every war has been the enemy of the ideas and technological innovations that its perpetrators utilized. Over the course of the Cold War, the use of various technologies, such as the rocket for nuclear missiles, contributed significantly to humanity's current and precarious state of affairs. Long before the advent of spacefaring technology and nuclear weapons, humanity cemented itself as a species that could adapt to rapid change, a trend that continues to this day, for better or for worse.

Only within the past few centuries has humanity begun to face the challenge of adapting, not to a hostile natural environment that our proficiency with tools can make appear subservient at times, but rather to the artificial, anthropocentric environments we find ourselves increasingly unable to escape. Giants of government and industry, as well as the populations of Earth's current nations, struggle to adapt to the playing fields of their various forbears, vast chessboards showing signs of mutation and decay. In this increasingly post-human environment, where the narratives underpinning culture receive overdue scrutiny, many have begun to criticize archetypes such as the "hero", elements of myth studied by scholars including Joseph Campbell and Carl Jung.

Considering myth from a critical perspective suggests that these narratives, while foundational to their respective societies of origin, are neither flawless examples of ideal moralities that should remain untouched by critical theory, nor wholly outdated and problematic tales that should be outright dismissed or derided. All myths are based on events experienced by diverse collectives of past humans who struggled to survive the unforgiving journey of life, and, as such, the thorough study of myth requires both our criticism and our consideration.

Lost cosmonauts and astronauts are the heroes (or, in many cases, the martyrs and scapegoats) of modernity's mythical expeditions into outer space, figures that remain central to propagandistic portrayals of American and Russian culture, respectively. Space exploration may have given rise to certain modern myths, from conspiracy theories surrounding the Apollo moon missions to the worship of UFOs, but, like all catalysts of myth, it does not offer a set of values or ideals in and of itself.

Ultimately, humanity creates and revises semantic systems in response to shifts in culture. Born from such fluctuations, new systems will always already be both imperfect and temporary. Vigorously critiquing the ever-amorphous systems we find ourselves in at any given moment, regardless of their seeming validity or completeness, remains our best defence against ignorance and exploitation.

Every time a myth emerges, the "bravery" of those labelled its heroes serves as a cover for the conditioning, coercion, and other social pressures that the humans beneath that label endured. Reassessing the hero narratives of cosmonauts and astronauts first requires humanizing them—unveiling their mortality and noting the human errors that contributed to their deaths deconstructs portrayals of these people as infallible heroes, as military icons, and as vanguards of scientific and military power.

Space exploration could have been a shared goal from the beginning, a co-operative effort between nations aimed at expanding knowledge and promoting peace. In the end, however, humanity showcased its most destructive and regressive qualities during the Space Race, all the while re-branding each mission as a victory, like tallies on a global chalkboard of cultural, military, and neocolonial posturing.

On this planet, our tragically self-destructive species continues to persist. Now that we are entering an era in which we have begun to make unprecedented efforts to re-evaluate ourselves, the first step to this new engagement with our past is to engage with its dead, and with the complexity of their complicity in both our idealistic myths and our far harsher reality.

APOSTLES OF ICARUS

This poem likens astronauts and cosmonauts who lost their lives during space missions to the ancient Greek mythical figure Icarus, who flew too close to the sun on wings glued together with wax. The wax melted, the wings fell apart, and Icarus fell into the ocean and drowned. The poem makes reference to the "lost cosmonauts" myth, believers of which claim the Soviet Union concealed the identities and deaths of several cosmonauts in the late 1950s and early 1960s.

THE SPACE RACE

This series of poems chronologically follows landmarks in the development of spacefaring technology, beginning with Russian thinker Konstantin Tsilokovsky's equations and engine component designs in the poem "Engine," written in terza rima in tribute to the metric form of Dante's Inferno. As a further nod to Dante, the poem considers the terrible potential of the knowledge that Tsilokovsky developed, by likening such discoveries to infernal secrets, their fruits used not only to explore space but to create more advanced missiles. The following poem, "Probes," celebrates the launch of the Voyager probes, both of which continue to send valuable data to NASA decades after their missions began. Probes consists of six haiku-based stanzas, the meditative form and careful construction of which echo the compact elegance of the Voyager probes. The third poem, "Capsules," is dedicated to Yuri Gagarin, the first man in space, and to Valentina Tereshkova, the first woman in space. The poem addresses both cosmonauts, highlighting the shared significance of their respective "first" flights.

The poem inhabits a blank-verse ghazal, an Arabic form traditionally invoked to portray unrequited love. This form was chosen not to suggest a romantic pairing of the two cosmonauts but rather to represent the unification of their two "firsts" "Station," the fourth poem in the series, echoes, in its concrete form, the shape of the linked living modules of the International Space Station. The fifth poem, "Offshoots," contemplates humanity's insatiable ability to adapt to harsh environments to evolve by challenging ourselves against the unknown, and to ultimately transcend our physical bodies to more resilient forms and achieve greater agency over our deaths.

VOYAGE TO LUNA

As renowned Canadian experimental poet Christian Bök noted in a 2013 *Maclean's* article, "had the ancient Greeks rowed a trireme (boat) to the Moon, you can bet there would be a 12-volume epic about that adventure." This section makes literal Bök's notion, chronicling the Apollo 8, 10, and 11 missions in a 12-part poem written in dactylic hexameter, the traditional form of the Greek epic. The long poem chronicles these three missions not from the perspectives of the astronauts involved, but rather from the viewpoints of the canon of major and minor Greco-Roman deities associated with the Moon. These deities observe mortal efforts to reach the Moon, deliberating over what should be done in lieu of such blasphemous acts.

THE KARDASHEV SCALE

This section contains a triptych of cantos in terza rima, and is named after Soviet astronomer Nikolai Kardashev. The chosen form invokes a kind of Dante-like descent into the strange Hell of speculative evolution, a journey that brings our species eerily far from all that we call "human." The poems follow the projected progression of civilization through three stages of development, based on total energy usage, according to the scale Kardashev developed in 1964. At the first stage, humanity has harnessed all energy available on Earth. The poem "Globus Cassus" presents a scenario in which humanity might achieve this stage, based on a concept developed by Swiss architect Christian Waldvogel in his 2004 book of the same name. At the second stage of the Kardashev scale, humanity has harnessed all of the sun's available energy. The poem "Dyson Sphere" explores a way in which we might accomplish this, by building a structure of the same name (originally conceived by Olaf Stapledon in his 1937 novel *Star Maker*). During the third stage of the Kardashev scale, whatever species humanity has evolved into has achieved the capability to harness energy on a galactic scale. The final poem of this section, "Galactic Engineering," explores numerous science-fiction concepts related to this theme, such as the 'new foreignness' of Earth, and how the post-human entities of the far future might respond to the threats of the cosmos, such as potentially apocalyptic asteroids and gamma ray bursts.

WAX WINGS

Thematically invoking the myth of Icarus, this section elegizes the deaths of all astronauts and cosmonauts killed during space missions (or in training exercises meant to prepare them for such missions). "Crucible," a modified sestina, contains an additional, prefacing stanza added to enhance the poem's symmetry. "Eye of Dawn," a free verse piece, meditates upon the eerie, ritualistic undertones of a photo taken prior to the Apollo 1 disaster. "Countdown" consists of ten stanzas, three lines each, to evoke the famous countdown from ten that heralds the launches of rockets. "Ezekiel 37:9" comments upon the demise of the crew of Soyuz 11 and "Fragment" upon the *Challenger* disaster, both using free verse. "Dark Mirrors" presents four square stanzas, each nine lines long, in order to represent the Space Mirror Memorial. "Red Phantoms" massages conspiracy theorists' accounts of lost cosmonaut transmissions into a series of haiku-based stanzas, tributes to English poetic efforts at emulating the Japanese form, in order to encapsulate the brevity and significance of the purported transmissions. Finally, "Causality" lists the causes of confirmed astronaut and cosmonaut deaths in non-spaceflight-related disasters and training mishaps.

CELESTIAL BODIES

These seven poems were inspired by the composer Gustav Holst's orchestral suite *The Planets*. The poems, named after the movements of Holst's suite, each take on distinct forms meant to evoke the character and characteristics of their respective companion deities from the ancient Greco-Roman pantheons. Desiccated, blood-rusted Mars is warlike, and "Venus" paradoxically peaceful, her surface environment so inhospitable that life would be unable to propagate there. These first two poems, a pair of ghazals in blank verse, echo the relationship between Mars and Venus as told by Greek mythology. "Mercury," sporadic and fleeting, pays tribute to the Japanese choka, its stanzas shaped like the wings adorning the shoes of the poem's god. "Jupiter" inhabits a sonnet, perhaps the most well-known poetic form, and fitting given Jupiter's role as an aged king. Saturn, the god of the harvest, time, and death, takes on the form of a villanelle, a nod to Dylan Thomas's poem "Do Not Go Gentle into that Good Night," which urges us to wring life dry in the face of death, to "harvest" each moment when ripe. "Uranus, the Magician," a modified sonnet, consists of fourteen blank verse lines, each a perfect anagram of the poem's title, including its single comma. "Neptune" revels in its sixteen stanzas, further tributes to haiku that collectively address the planet's presently catalogued moons, linking them to the nymphs for which they were named while briefly describing the personae and history of each water deity.

ORBITAL DEBRIS

This section of three found poems begins with "In Event of Moon Disaster," a Nixon-era contingency letter composed by speech writer William Safire, for use in case the crew of

Apollo 11 were unable to return to Earth. "In the Shadow of the Moon" re-presents a Reddit post made by Buzz Aldrin during an AMA on October 30th, 2014, in which Aldrin describes his state-of-mind as the Apollo capsule approached the Moon. "Last Words" is composed solely of the final words spoken by astronauts and cosmonauts who perished on their way to space, or during spaceflight. "Prepare/cognac and sausage to go/with the moonshine /see you tomorrow" was spoken by various members of the Soyuz 11 crew, during their final transmission before their voyage home. "Roger, uh, bu–" is the last audio transmission from the *Columbia* shuttle, spoken by mission commander Rick Husband. "Uh-oh" is the final transmission received from the *Challenger* shuttle, uttered by Michael Smith. "Get us out" was the last phrase heard during the fire of Apollo 1. "It was my fault/no one else/is to blame" were the last words of Valentin Bondarenko, before his death several hours later.

BEYOND THE INFINITE

This section speculates upon as-of-yet indescribable and indefinable aspects of the universe, phenomena such as dark matter, dark energy, black holes, extra dimensions, and other puzzles of physics, comparing these phenomena to the sublime experience of attempting to comprehend one's simultaneous insignificance and profound rarity as a living, conscious being. The first three poems are written in blank, free verse. "Pale Blue Dot" begins by gesturing toward the Moon landing as a uniquely self-reflexive moment in our collective history, when humanity's perception of itself and of Earth was irrevocably altered. "Astral Vagabond" chronicles the transition of Syrian astronaut Muhammed Faris from his military position to that of a refugee, after his defection from Syria in 2012. "Space Poem Chain" pairs a translation of astronaut Koichi Wakata's 2009 poem of the same title, and the first poem written in outer space, with a line-by-line anagram response to the translation. "Per Aspera Ad Astra" ("through hardship to the stars") chronicles humanity's history of, and propensity for, exploration, which has proved both a boon and a curse. "Antiverse Palindrome" is an English translation of a Russian poem by Mikhail Pukhov. This translation retains the original poem's word-based palindromic form while rewriting the poem as a canto in terza rima, likening the plight of the poem's fictional astronauts to that of Dante. "The Passage Lies Here" is a tribute to Canadian poet Gwendolyn MacEwen, who wrote several poems about the Apollo missions during the time of their occurrence.

Notes & Acknowledgements

The Lost Cosmonauts was not a project I undertook lightly. I extend my utmost gratitude to the following friends and colleagues for their various, gracious contributions to this book: derek beaulieu, Gregory Betts, Christian Bök, Stephanie Bolster, Stephen Cain, Jay MillAr, Darren Wershler, Sina Queyras, Kate Marshall, and each one of the students enrolled in Concordia University's English 672 workshop class of 2015/16. Finally, I offer my utmost love and thanks to my family for their generous support, and to my partner Nicole Pucci, my unwavering co-pilot.

The poem "Pale Blue Dot" was printed by Christian Bök's micro-press Chromium Dioxide, as a part of the limited edition of *The Xenotext: Book I*. Additionally, the poems "Apostles of Icarus" and "Antiverse Palindrome" appeared as chapbooks available from derek beaulieu's No Press.

The Lost Cosmonauts is dedicated to the following astronauts and cosmonauts, may they rest in peace: Vladimir Komarov, Georgi Dobrovolski, Viktor Patsayev, Vladislav Volkov, Gregory Jarvis, Christa McAuliffe, Ronald McNair, Ellison Onizuka, Judith Resnik, Michael Smith, Dick Scobee, Rick Husband, William McCool, Michael Anderson, David Brown, Kalpana Chawla, Laurel Clark, Ilan Ramon, Michael Adams, Valentin Bondarenko, Theodore Freeman, Elliot See, Charles Bassett, Virgil Grissom, Edward White, Roger Chaffee, Clifton Williams, Robert Lawrence, Yuri Gagarin, Vladimir Seryogin, Sergei Vozovikov, and Michael Alsbury.

KEN HUNT'S written work has appeared in *Chromium Dioxide*, *Freefall*, No Press, Spacecraft Press, *Rampike*, and *Matrix*, as well as in the poetry anthology *The Calgary Renaissance*. His first book of poetry, *Space Administration*, was published in 2014 by the LUMA Foundation, as the third book of poetry in Hans Ulrich and Kenneth Goldsmith's *89+ Project*. For three years, Ken served as managing editor of *NōD Magazine*, and for one year, he served as poetry editor of *filling Station*. In 2014, Ken founded Spacecraft Press, a micro-press specializing in writing inspired by science and technology. Ken is pursuing a PhD at Western University.